MASTERS IN

D1176420

# VAN GOGH

*Distributed in the U. S. A. and Canada*
*by*
CROWN PUBLISHERS
419 FOURTH AVENUE NEW YORK, N. Y.

LA MOUSME detail Arles period
National Gallery of Art, Washington, D.C. Chester Dale Collection (Lo

HYPERION MINIATURES

# VAN GOGH

BY

ANDRE LECLERC

THE HYPERION PRESS

NEW YORK . PARIS . LONDON

*SHOES, Paris period, Vallotton Art Gallery Lausanne*

# VAN GOGH

THE originality of Van Gogh lies in his direct and intense vision, his symbolic use of color, which as he used to say, "in itself expresses some-hing," and his construction, inspired by Japanese art. His masters are embrandt, Rubens and Delacroix, whose influence, together with that of any other greatly different painters, he melted into work which, with ézanne's, is perhaps the most individual creation of our time.

Born on March 30th, 1853, at Groot-Zundert in Holland, Vincent van ogh was the eldest of six children. His father was a minister and his up-inging, in an atmosphere of poverty and stern idealism, went a long way wards moulding his quixotic personality. His childhood and adolescence showed no promise of talent but unmistakable signs of an abnormal nature. He shunned his brothers and sisters, all but Theodore, "Theo," four years younger than himself, who worshipped his elder brother and never failed him later in life. Until the age of twelve, Vincent spent most of his time roaming about the countryside; he achieved no notable success in his studies at Zevenbergen, a little town near his native village, where he lived the next four years. At sixteen he was sent to The Hague on the recommendation of his uncle, a former associate of the firm of Goupil which dealt in pictures and had branches in London and Paris, for employment as a clerk in that establishment. When at the age of twenty he was promoted to the London branch, he began to draw, partly impelled by the influence of the pictures which passed through his hands, partly to while away time. Two years later he fell in love with the daughter of his landlady, but the young girl turned him down. The disappointment created an inferiority complex which influenced Vincent's whole life and is a major factor in the evolution of his art.

Such was the change in Vincent's nature as a result of his unhappy love affair, that his employers found him unbearable and dismissed him. Vincent turned to religion for succour. After a few months of work as an assistant-teacher at Ramsgate and Isleworth, he decided to become a preacher. However, neither his education nor his powers of elocution fitted him for this calling and he was not permitted to continue. He then tried to prepare a university entrance examination in Amsterdam, but being unused to study, soon gave up the attempt. Sponsored by an evangelical society which required no diplomas, he went as lay preacher to the mining district of the Borinage in Belgium. There, in a effort to save the rough miners souls, he made himself conspicuous by living literally up to his creed, giving away his miserable allowance, sleeping on the floor in an old hut with a leaking roof, publicly confessing his own sins, with no result save that of being jeered at and finally dismissed.

The period in the Borinage, though apparently another failure, was the starting point of Vincent's evolution as a painter. It was there that he began to draw in real earnest, seeing in his as yet crude but already forceful art a means of glorifying God and spreading the Gospel by expressing the life of toil and poverty led by the people around him. As yet he had no attemted to paint; that was to come later.

He led the life of a tramp, wandering about the mining districts and the countryside, drawing, preaching, sometimes returning home. It was Theo who out of his small earnings spared a little allowance for his erran

THE POTATO EATERS detail Nuenen period
Collection V. W. Van Gogh, Amsterdam          [7]

*THE IRON BRIDGE AT TRINQUETAILLE*
*Arles period, Coll. Sonja Kramarsky, N. Y.*

brother. Another year passed. At last the family decided to give him
fresh start in the career he seemed to have chosen, and he was sent to Bru
sels with a small subsidy, to study art.

All went well for about a year. Vincent made progress, met interesti
people and felt happier. In a hard-working mood, he returned to his parer
then resident at Etten, who seemed far more sympathetic now that he show
signs of having settled down. But catastrophe lay in store for him; a cous
with whom he fell in love rejected his advances; there was another brea
with his environment and Vincent left for The Hague. There he quarrel

*THE ANGLOIS BRIDGE Arles period*
*Kroller-Muller Foundation, Hoenderlo*

with his teacher, the painter Mauve, and to crown the strangeness of his
conduct, picked up a woman of the streets and devoted himself to her. Her
name was Sien; it is her spent, emaciated body that he depicted in *Sorrow*
which she seemed to incarnate to his idealistic eyes. The woman proved
absolutely worthless, but he stayed with her for nearly two years and it was
Theodore who, much against his brother's will, persuaded her by means of
a bribe to leave the poor sick man, then in hospital as result of malnutrition
and general neglect.

*SEA-VIEW AT SAINTES-MARIES Arles period*
*Museum of Modern Art, Moscow*

Vincent slowly recovered, first alone at Drenthe where, in a better frame of mind, he spent the summer painting landscapes, then at Nuenen, where he found refuge in winter, his father then being minister of the little town. For the third time a woman upset the precarious balance of Vincent's life; this time it was she who, strangely enough, fell in love with the awkward, bad-tempered, disreputable man, and finding him indifferent tried to commit suicide. Vincent absorbed himself in work and painted some of his finest pictures: *The Potato-Eaters, Potatoes* —he was haunted by the symbolic humility, apart from the quaint shape, of this vegetable— *Boots* and many variants on the theme of the hard-working peasantry. He painted in dark, sunless colors, and his idea was to convey the very smell of poverty, rusticity and ceaseless toil.

At Antwerp, Vincent made two discoveries which, irrelevant to each other though they may seem, both influenced his painting profoundly. The first was Rubens, the second, absolutely new, was the art of the Japanese which the novels of the Goncourt brothers had recently brought into vogue. The light, sunny colors and bright red contours of Rubens changed Vincent's outlook entirely, while the prints of Hokusai and Hiroshighe encouraged him not only in the use of bold, primary colors, strongly contrasted, but also of an asymmetrical and conventionally spontaneous style of composition. Vincent seemed to have settled down to work in peace; however, after several months study at the Antwerp Academy, he persuaded Theo that it would be cheaper to let him live in Paris where the younger brother was in steady employment.

There seemed to be no better atmosphere for Vincent than that of Paris with its museums and cafés. He tried to study again under a teacher, Cormon, but with his usual impatience gave it up and decided that henceforward he needed no master. He persevered and when he met Gauguin, Toulouse-Lautrec and Seurat, it was with the sense of being their equal. He painted Montmartre and the suburbs of Paris; he also painted the humblest things that met his eye; rickety chairs and sardine-tins, as in the old days when his subjects had been boots and potatoes. He met Père Tanguy, the odd dealer in colors and pictures who had set Cézanne on the road to fame by selling his works at so much per square inch and cutting them up if necessary. Vincent's pictures did not sell and Cézanne, whom he whole-heartedly admired, disliked him intensely.

As was to be foreseen, Vincent soon tired of Paris, disagreeing with everybody and making himself unbearable. In 1887, on the advice of Toulouse-Lautrec, he left for the south of France. His violent and unpredictable moods had made his faithful brother glad to be rid of him, but he continued to write long, affectionate letters full of little sketches with indications of color. He was entranced by the sunshine and the radiant countryside at Arles, so different from the grey of his native Holland, and he painted the vast expanses of sunlit fields and meadows in the plain of the Crau, giving within the narrow limits of his canvas an extraordinary sense of space. He still liked to paint portraits and people, expressing by the use of violent contrasts of color, between his sitter and the background for instance, not only the character of his model but also, deliberately, his own feelings in regard to the person, whether he were the postman, a peasant or a friend. He also tried to paint the unpaintable; night and the starry sky, in whirls of yellow and blue.

His unhappy fate was not, however, to be shaken off. It all began with a fine project, in keeping with Vincent's old idealism. This was to found a community of painters, all working together in harmony and collaborating in the execution of a masterpiece. He invited Gauguin, who came and actually stayed for two months, at the end of which occurred the tragi-comedy that comes across the mind whenever the name of Van Gogh is mentioned. The two friends quarrelled about their art, Vincent suddenly threw a glass at Gauguin, and the next day, after a period of calm, threatened him with a razor. Then, in a spirit of self-chastisement, Vincent cut off one of his own ears.

He was placed in a mental institution at Saint-Rémy, where he painted the grounds, the keeper, the physician, and was found harmless enough. The treatment did him little good, however, and he was let out after a year. He then went to live at Auvers-sur-Oise, near Paris, where he painted the portrait of Dr. Gachet, a lover of art who really understood his case and who taught him the technique of engraving. At Auvers, Vincent seemed happy and calm.

In the meantime, during the year at Saint-Rémy, an article by Albert Aurier appeared in the Mercure de France, drawing attention to the work of Van Gogh. It was recognition at last, but Vincent no longer really cared. His fragile health was undermined by senseless remorse and despair. On July 27th, 1890, without any explanation but following doubtless some inner logic of his own, he attempted to shoot himself and died two days later of the wound.

Theo survived him but for a year; his death was caused by paralysis consequent upon the shock of his brother's suicide.

Art springing from a pathetically unbalanced altruistic impulse, yet ultimately neither mawkish nor literary art, but a straighforward statement without comment in a new intensity of vision, such is the achievement of Van Gogh who died a lucid madman after having lived like an irrational saint.

ANDRE LECLERC

PORTRAIT OF THE SUPERINTENDENT OF
ST. PAUL'S HOSPITAL St. Remy period

[13]

FRITILLARIES IN A COPPER VASE Paris period
Louvre Museum, Paris.

STILL LIFE, IRISES St. Remy period
Collection V. W. Van Gogh

PORTRAIT OF A PEASANT Nuenen period
Bernheim Jeune Art Gallery, Paris

PORTRAIT OF THE ARTIST IN A STRAW HAT Paris period
The Detroit Institute of Arts                    [17]

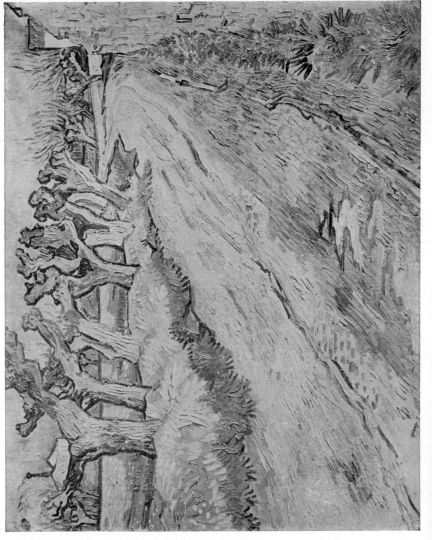

HOUSES AT AUVERS  Auvers period
Toledo Museum of Art, Ohio

[19]

[20]  SELF PORTRAIT Arles period Collection Berheim Jeune, Paris.

PEASANT WOMAN WEARING A FRILLED BONNET
Nuenen period. Collection Madame Flemming, London     [21]

THE REAPER (After Millet) Saint-Remy period
Collection V. W. Van Gogh, Amsterdam

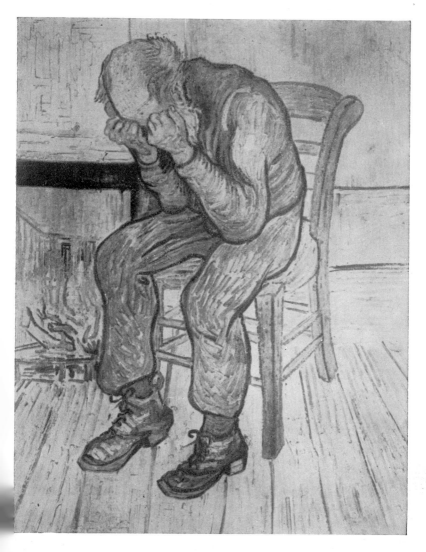

ON THE THRESHOLD OF ETERNITY Saint-Remy period
Kroller-Muller Foundation                    [23]

THE WOMAN WITH THE TAMBOURINES Paris Period
Collection V. W. Van Gogh

PERE TANGUY Paris period
Collection Edward G. Robinson, Beverly Hills          [25]

THE RUBY OF THE KING Arles period
Knoedler Art Gallery, New York

THE PRISON COURTYARD  Saint-Remy  period
Museum of Modern Art, Moscow          [27]

THE FARM GATE Arles period
Private Collection, Paris

THE BRIDGE AT ASNIERES Paris period
Collection F. H. Hirchlnad, New York

HOUSES AT AUVERS Auvers period John T. Spaulding, Boston [31]

HEAD OF A PEASANT WITH A PIPE Nuenen period
Kroller-Muller Foundation, Hoenderlo

PORTRAIT OF HIMSELF Paris period
Collection V. W. Van Gogh

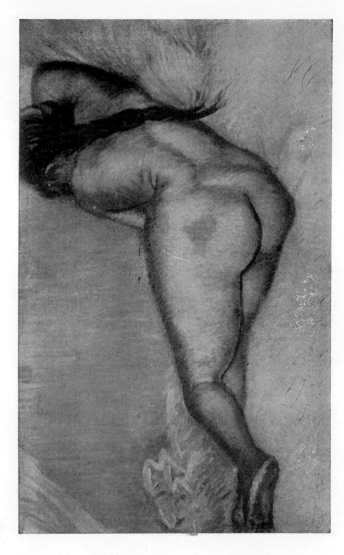

NUDE WOMAN RECLINING Paris period
Collection Mme. L. Reinach-Goujon, Paris

THE STEVEDORES Arles period, Collection Carleton Mitchell, Chevy Chase, Md.

LA MOUSME Arles period National Gallery of Art,
Washington D. C. Chester Dale Collection. (Loan)

THE MAN WITH THE CORNFLOWER Auvers period
Collection Mendelssohn-Bartholdy, Berlin          [37]

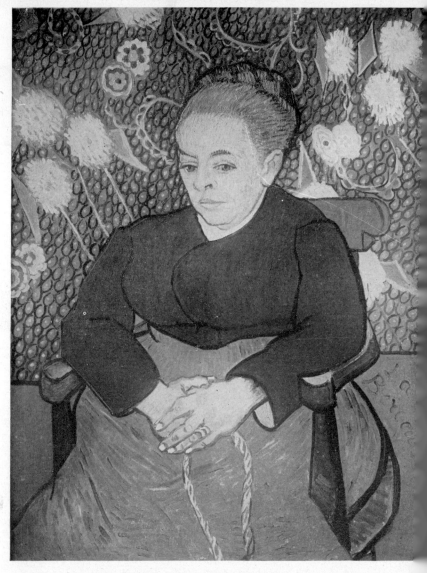

LA BERCEUSE (MADAME ROULIN) Arles period
Paul Rosenberg Art Gallery, Paris

PORTRAIT OF DOCTOR REY Arles period
Museum of Modern Art, Moscow                    [39]

MONTMARTRE Paris period The Art Institute of Chicago,
Helen Birch Bartlett Memorial Collection

THE CAFE AT NIGHT Arles period
Kroller-Muller Foundation. Hoenderlo

PORTRAIT OF ARMAND ROULIN detail Arles period
Folkwang Museum, Essen

THE SCHOOLBOY St. Remy period
Collection M. Meirowsky, Berlin

SHEEP-SHEARERS (after Millet) Saint Remy period
Collection V. W. Van Gogh

MADEMOISELLE GACHET AT THE PIANO Auvers period
Basle Museum, Dr. P. Gachet's Collection          [45]

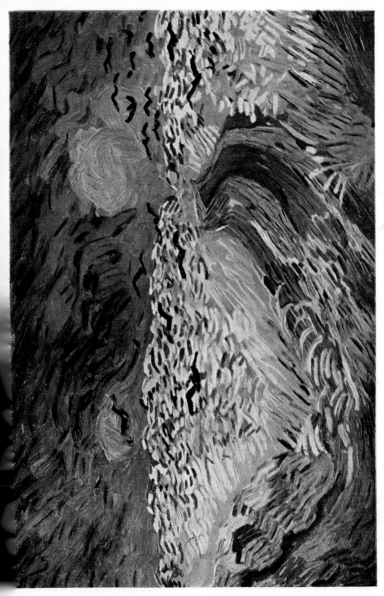

CROWS ON THE CORNFIELD detail Auvers period
Collection V. W. Van Gogh, Amsterdam